HARE PIE SCR
& BOTTLE K

HALLATON'S STRANGE ANI

CONTENTS

ABOVE: At the Buttercross the decorated bottles are held aloft by L-R: Michael Hunt, The Master of the Stowe Phil Allan and Simon Bull. The Warrener John Morison with the ceremonial Hare, Jane Johnson carries the two dozen Penny Loaves, Susan Allan and Sharon Hunt hold the sacks containing the Hare Pie. 1996

INTRODUCTION

Bottle Kicking, a sport older than Rugby, older than cricket, older than the Real Tennis of Henry VIII's court, is possibly a distant ancestor of football. It is a rough and tough game played just once a year, deep in the rolling English countryside. This strange and dangerous game and associated Hare Pie Scrambling takes place each Easter Monday, in the village of Hallaton in Leicestershire. It all started many centuries ago, pre-dating the evidence of seventeenth century records. Life in medieval England is known to have included many such celebrations and events and no doubt this local tradition has its origins in much earlier times.

What then is the recipe for this rustic conflict? Beer in small barrels (known as Bottles), a Hare Pie and Penny Loaves are the edible ingredients, accompanied by pageantry, music and a church service. These are brought together with a heady concoction of pride, passion and virility. Easter Monday is the day for fun and fighting, for family gatherings, for vigorous rivalry and unruly brawling. Such is the essence of the exciting, curious and ancient custom of Hare Pie Scrambling and Bottle Kicking. *

The neighbouring villages of Hallaton and Medbourne are located in the southeastern corner of Leicestershire. For just one day each year the friendly relationship that exists between them is put aside and a much older and darker hostility breaks out. On Easter Monday the villagers and their supporters come together on a hill top. There they engage in fierce competition; in a rough and roudy battle to scamble for a pie and to wrestle a cask of ale back to their own village.

Correctly referred to as Hare Pie Scrambling and Bottle Kicking, the custom is commonly termed in an abbreviated form as "Bottle Kicking". Though using this shorter term we must emphasise that Bottle Kicking is just one part of the long established custom.

ORDER OF EVENTS

9.30 am	BAND WILL PLAY AT MEDBOURNE
10.30 am	CHILDRENS PARADE LED BY THE BAND FROM THE BEWICKE ARMS TO ST MICHAEL'S CHURCH, HALLATON
11.00 am	BOTTLE KICKING SERVICE IN ST MICHAEL'S CHURCH, HALLATON ①
From 12.00	REFRESHMENTS AVAILABLE IN STENNING HALL
1.00 pm	BAND WILL PLAY AT THE VILLAGE GREEN (WEATHER PERMITTING)
1.45pm	PARADE OF THE BOTTLES AND HARE PIE FROM THE FOX INN TO THE CHURCH GATES ②
2.00pm	CUTTING UP AND DISTRIBUTING OF THE HARE PIE AT THE CHURCH GATES ③
2.10pm	DRESSING THE BOTTLES AT THE VILLAGE GREEN ④ AND DISTRIBUTION OF THE PENNY LOAVES ⑤
2.45pm	BOTTLE KICKING MARCH FROM THE FOX INN TO HARE PIE BANK ⑥
3.00pm	THE HARE PIE SCRAMBLE ⑦ AND THE START OF THE BOTTLE KICKING AT HARE PIE BANK ⑧
	AFTER THE CONTEST COME AND SEE THE CONQUERING HEROES CELEBRATE AT THE BUTTERCROSS ⑨

MAP OF EVENTS

THE FOX INN

North End

② Parade of the Bottles

⑥ March to Hare Pie Bank

THE BEWICKE ARMS

High Street

① The Service

Church Gate

THE BUTTERCROSS

ST MICHAEL'S

④ Dressing the Bottles

⑤ The Penny Loaves

⑨ Victory Celebrations

③ Cutting the Hare Pie

Bride Hill

stream

HARE PIE BANK

⑦ The Hare Pie Scramble

⑧ The Bottle Kicking

THE CEREMONY

EASTER MONDAY MORNING

In the quiet and charming villages of Medbourne and Hallaton, the year-long peacefulness is disrupted by the Easter Monday festivities.

In both villages, there are arrangements for handling a huge influx of visitors. The pubs have come to expect hoards of young people. Landlords who have long since learned to stack away removable and breakable items and gear up to provide outside service under canvas. Battle-dressed contestants seek out fellow players to share beers and comradeship. Others eager to attend but hesitant to play may get swept along on a tide of enthusiasm and ready ale. The all-day Pubs have a demanding day but stock up for their biggest sales opportunity of the year.

At Hallaton, the first public celebration of Easter Monday is the Children's Parade. At around 10.30am, the band starts to play on the village green, encouraging the youngsters to come along and join the procession. As the band plays and leads the way from The Cross, the children fall in behind. They march past the Bewicke Arms around Eastgate and up through North End to the Fox Inn. By then with a few more supporters, the parade continues its circuit down the High Street and back to The Cross. However few the followers, the Childrens' Parade is a charming preliminary to the annual festivities.

The band plays and the crowds gather. Among them there are likely to be many repeat visitors, family visitors and guests, and even guests of guests. This major event of the year provides a focus for family reunions and for many, the chance to renew old acquaintances. Housewives in the village may not know who or even how many will come: They will be prepare though, with tables stocked with hams, tongues, pork-pies, salads, potatoes and gallons of tea. They are ready for any numbers of invited or uninvited guests. Many of the visitors may come with little or no prior knowledge of the events but with interest and curiosity about the strange custom.

Hallaton Band ready outside the Old Royal Oak. The members of the Friendly Societies are to the rear holding their staffs of office. 1905

The peal of bells of the church of St Michael & All Angels announces the traditional Bottle Kicking Service. At 11.00am, the Rector welcomes the procession leaders. First comes the Warrener in medieval costume, holding aloft the bronze hare. Also in period costume comes the Bread Lady, carrying the basket of Penny Loaves. Next come the two carriers of the sacks for the Hare Pie and finally the Bottles, held high, by the Master of the Stowe and the two other honoured bottle holders. The Rector greets them at the high altar and takes the symbols offered. The church service follows, to which all comers are welcome and which by ancient tradition includes a sermon relevant to the day. After the last rousing hymn, the officials collect the artefacts from around the altar and lead the congregation from the church to join the gathering crowds.

The banner of the Loyal Farmers Delight Lodge of the Oddfellows leads the procession from the Church Service in 1907.

PARADE OF THE BOTTLES

After the service, while some take lunch, others seek the liquid refreshment at the village pubs displaying "Ale Bushes".

The Ale Bush was a sign that ale was for sale. This custom was common in the middle ages and is a relic from Roman times. By ancient law and tradition, private houses were permitted to brew ale for sale on feast days and special occasions. These houses were known as Bough Houses and were required to display Ale Bushes.

There are no longer any local Bough Houses but both villages still have two pubs to meet the needs of bottle kickers and visitors.

By early afternoon Hallaton is buzzing with activity and an air of excitement. Hundreds of visitors have arrived. The police have closed off the roads to all vehicles except the emergency services. Local and national press are represented and many television recordings have been made. There is much interest from abroad, with films and tele-recordings of the event for audiences world-wide. Visiting celebrities are not unusual.

Among those who have attended in recent decades are Chris Brasher, Athlete and TV Presenter, Chris Searle of TV fame and the World Heavyweight Boxing champion Frank Bruno.

Though there is this wide interest, the Hare Pie Scrambling and Bottle Kicking is still very much a local affair. There are strong feelings of loyalty and commitment among the locals that outsiders may find difficulty to understand.

The procession leaders and followers gather outside the Fox Inn at North End. The police clear a way through the crowds. The band strikes up and the parade begins. Leading the procession are the ceremonial officials. The Warrener carries the Hare on a Pole and heads the other carriers; of the Penny Loaves, the Hare Pie and the sacks for the pie and the all-important bottles. The bottles are heavy but are held high with pride throughout the long parade. The crowds lining the streets join in the procession as it passes, milling and jostling for position.

L-R: Ivan Read carries one the sacks, Bottle Carrier Cat Weasel a professional booth wrestler, Mrs Edith Payne with the Hare Pie, Master of the Stowe "Wacka" Wainwright holds the dummy, Mick Garfield right hand Bottle, Mrs Bet Marsden, daughter of Sporty Payne holds the Pie. City of Leicester Pipe Band. 1975

Noisily progressing down the High Street, the procession pauses in silent respect outside the building that was until recently The Royal Oak. There many generations of Bottle Kickers have prepared themselves for the frays of the past.

The parade comes to a halt at the gates to the churchto be greeted by the Rector. The crowd fills the roads and pathways and spills over into the churchyard. While some people seek vantage points from the churchyard walls, others cautiously watch from the adjacent houses.

The procession passing the Bede House, Church Street on its way to the Rectory to collect the Hare Pie. 1930

CUTTING THE HARE PIE

After blessing the Hare Pie and giving thanks, the Rector now performs the ritual duty of cutting the pie. To the cheers of the crowd and the flashing of cameras the great pie is cut into manageable pieces. While most of the pie is placed in the sacks for distribution later, some pieces are handed out to those within reach. This is when the lucky ones in the pressing crowd get their first taste of the Easter delicacy. For those further away, more pieces of pie are tossed over the heads of those nearby, for others in the crowd to catch. The pie is delicious and clean catches make for good eating. Inevitably, some of the pie falls to the ground, after which it is likely to take on a new form as a messy missile.

The procession reforms and is now joined by the Rector. The band strikes up and the whole company heads back to "The Cross".

The local name for the village green is The Cross and arises from the curious conical stone "buttercross" that stands on the green. The buttercross was the focal point of the market in medieval times when Hallaton was the centre of trade for this part of the East Midlands.

The bottle holders climb onto the stone seats around the buttercross and the Rector advances to "dress the bottles". In this ceremony, the Rector ties a special red, white and blue ribbon around each of the bottles and at both ends. The two sacks containing the Hare Pie are also sealed and tied with the ribbons.

Ready to cut the Hare Pie by the Church gates. L-R: George Fowles (Village Coalman) with sack, Mrs Edith Payne (maker of the pie), Rev W Chantler, Rector of Hallaton, his son, "Wacka" Wainwright with bottle, Mick Garfield. 1964

THE TWO DOZEN PENNY LOAVES

Gill Clayton with two dozen Penny Loaves. 1999

Another part of the ceremony now takes place on the green. Traditionally, two dozen penny loaves were given to the needy of the parish. With the absence of real poverty in Hallaton the need has long passed. However the tradition of distributing bread has been maintained. Many more loaves than the nominal two dozen are now provided. Freshly baked and tasty, they are eagerly sought by the children and adults alike.

During these ceremonies, many in the crowd will take advantage of the nearby Bewicke Arms to replenish their glasses. The mood is festive and good natured and people willingly move aside to allow the procession to reform for the march up the High Street to the Fox Inn.

The procession arrives to join an existing crowd and spreads over the traffic-free roads of North End and into the grounds of The Fox Inn. While many take the opportunity for yet another drink, others mill around, talking, exchanging greetings, making new friends, seeking acquaintances or just waiting and watching.

THE MARCH TO HARE PIE BANK

As the band strikes up, the bottles are raised high by men from both Medbourne and Hallaton. The crown is eager to commence. The whole colourful body of participants and protagonists surges forward gathering crowds as it passes down the High Street.

In Churchgate it passes No 8, the former home of one John Garner. He was infamous for breaking with traditional views of fair play by sweeping up the bottle whilst on horseback and galloping away crossing the stream to win the day for Hallaton.

Passing the church, down Church Lane and over Church Bridge, the parade then starts its steep climb up Bride Hill. On the way up the hill the band plays the tune "Old Easter Monday" The tune however, is more widely recognised as "The Grand Old Duke of York". The crowd sings and chants the words:-

Easter Monday is the day,
for Hallaton for fun
to see the club-folk go to church,
the lads and the lasses run.

At the top of the hill, the parade turns left into the field known as Hare Pie Bank, where a crowd has already gathered. Many will have taken the short-cut through the narrow jitty known as Tenters. The high ground is soon covered with people, with some youngsters seeking vantage points in the trees and on top of fences.

Only a slight depression in the ground within a rectangular ridge distinguishes the starting place of the contest. With the crowds now assembled the scramble for the Hare Pie begins. Two sacks containing the Hare Pie are held at both ends between the two nominated carriers. They swing the sacks in an arc, releasing the open ends so as to catapult the pieces of pie into the air and towards the outstretched hands of the crowd.

A boisterous crowd well fortified with ale, head past the Village Green on their way to the main event of the day. 1954

Up Bride Hill on the way to Hare Pie Bank. The Rectory and St Michael's Church in the background. L-R: Simon Bull of Churchgate with bottle, Michael Summers of Fern Farm with the dummy, Will Jackson, Ian Green of Hallaton Farm with bottle, Gilbert from Welham. 1990

The lucky ones catch pieces and enjoy them, whilst others treat the delight with less respect.

The weather certainly affects many of the activities of the day but is no bar to the main event taking place. Hare Pie Scrambling & Bottle Kicking has withstood the ordeals of driving snow and soaring summer temperatures. So what if conditions do make Hare Pie Bank somewhat inhospitable? These are minor deterrents. The customs have continued in spite of much greater challenges of dispute and deprivation and through the dark years of war.

George Neal and Walter Brown throw up the Hare Pie, 1924

THE CONTEST

This peculiar event is the big occasion of the year. Loving the excitement, the dangers and the camaraderie of the battle, regulars come along to join the villagers in the scramble. Others less daring, will push and shove from the fringes as they enter the spirit of the contest. Many more will come just to watch the rough game.

LET BATTLE COMMENCE!

The enthusiasm and energy of those about to play this game would astound an uninformed observer. The combatants really care about the contest and willingly risk their limbs for the chance to get the Bottle. So what makes people engage in this

reckless pursuit, year after year? Adding to the inherent aggressiveness of youth there is a sense of pride and partisanship, of loyalty and commitment. An indication of the level of aggressiveness and commitment comes from an incident in the 1930s related in "Step by Step" the autobiography of an old Hallatonian, Jack Stamp.

As the ring of battlers waited for the first bottle to be thrown up, a certain Hallaton man known as "Butcher" Marlow said "Lets start off as we mean to go on". He then proceeded to thump each of the Medbourne men in the face. He had dealt with quite a number of opponents before his progress was arrested in no uncertain manner.

The commitment of Butcher and the rest of the Marlows was well matched by the family Burrows of Medbourne. Along with Drivers, Swains, Smiths and Snows and many others they made a formidable team that dominated the contest in the middle of 20th century. Hallaton also had its strong men, well represented among others, by the families Payne, Stamp, White, Neal and Butteriss.

The scene is set and the contestants are fired up and ready for the fray. Tradition dictates that the Master of the Stowe takes the bottle and throws it high in the air, shouting "Bottle One" The surrounding contestants hold back. For "Bottle Two" the process is repeated. Then at "Bottle Three", as it falls to the ground, dozens of bodies pile upon the bottle and each other in an enormous scrum. Each player frantically tries to grab the bottle. Invisible beneath this seething heap of humanity there is someone holding the bottle. Well and truly locked within the writhing mass of arms, legs, hands, heads and bodies, somewhere there is a bottle that seems quite unlikely to emerge.

The real battle has begun.

LEFT: Bottle Three about to be hurled to the ground by "Wacka" Wainwright, c.1970

George Hill the Hallaton Blacksmith shows Bottle One. To his right hand Ted Hawke waiting expectantly. To his left Charlie Butteriss, c.1899

CONVENTIONS

In a contest in which there are no written rules, the locals know the object and conventions of the game. Others may need some enlightenment.

The contestants aim to take the bottle from Hare Pie Bank over countryside, crossing hedges and fences where necessary, to get it across the boundary stream to their own village. In Hallaton's case the home boundary is the brook that runs just to the south of the village. For the men from Medbourne, they must cross another brook far to the South, that runs from Slawston to Medbourne. With the steeper slope and a much shorter distance to their boundary stream, Hallaton always has an advantage. Medbourne has a greater distance and gentler slope. They have another disadvantage to overcome. To move towards their own stream, they must first cross the two hedges that line the Slawston bridleway.

11

By convention the bottle may be carried, rolled, kicked or thrown. Despite the peculiar title of the event, wrestling, pushing and carrying the bottle are more usual practices than kicking. Participants know that no form of transport may be utilised and that no weapons are allowed. Whilst accepting the inherent dangers of the fight, contestants will not tolerate apparel that can inflict injury. They quickly exclude anyone wearing spiked or studded boots and bar the use of special protection such as hard hats or crash helmets.

There is no limit on the numbers who may participate. There are no restrictions on who takes part, when they join in or when they leave the fray. The numbers do not have to be evenly matched and rarely are. There are no uniforms, kits, colours or numbering to identify teams. Only behaviour discloses the allegiances. More disconcerting for the cautious, there is no segregation nor division of territory between participants and spectators. It is open to all-comers. Everyone who willingly or unwillingly gets involved in the struggle becomes a combatant.

Once a bottle is won, there is a short respite for players to recover and return to the top of the hill. There the fight is continued with the second bottle. This is a dummy bottle made of solid wood and hence it is much lighter than the real bottles. Should the first and second bottle be won by opposing villages, a third contest is held as a decider.

With no referee, no umpire and no time limits, the only control of play is the discipline that is exercised by the participants themselves. Respect for the time-honoured traditions has been passed down and sustained through the centuries. This rough, rural game survives and thrives because it still entails a shared commitment to fair-play.

BATTLEFIELD SCENES

The scrum writhes and churns as combatants strive to get hold of the bottle. The whole throng struggles forwards, backwards and side to side in no clear pattern. The crowd presses all around until suddenly there is a break. A combatant emerges with the bottle. Scattering onlookers, he is oblivious to resistance and charges through such minor obstacles as barbed wire fences and hedges. The crowd quickly divides as spectators scream and flee from the danger. Opponents extract themselves from the pile of bodies to give chase. Such breaks rarely last long. Soon the man with the bottle is dragged down and becomes the nucleus of yet another scrum.

Running scrummage on Hare Pie Bank, c.1899

Everybody piles in and the massive scrum writhes again. Though most of those in the scrum are men, the outer layers are liable to include a few women and youngsters whose enthusiasm has overpowered their discretion. From apparent stalemate, a breakaway will sometimes catch the opponents off guard. Advances will be made before troops can reinforce the defence. Bottle Kicking consists of a series of scrums between occasional breakaways and running mauls.

TOP RIGHT: A mass scrummage in the early 1970s. looking down towards Hallaton village

BOTTOM RIGHT: The Bottle is down under a pile of bodies, 1994

THE CONTEST

Strong muscles help to protect a combatant crushed at the bottom of the heap of struggling humanity. Then the cry of "Man down" is heard as someone is seen to have succumbed to the overwhelming pressure. Sometimes people are pulled out of the scrum exhausted, only for their places to be taken by a seemingly endless supply of replacements. The moving scrum will leave in its wake a trail of prone participants. As one victim after another is dragged out the cry is "Bring out the dead!" Usually, with large gulps of fresh air and a brief rest, the restored player is straining to get back into the action.

When first-aiders first became involved there was an amusing incident. As they eagerly tended the "casualties" and stretchered them to the ambulance, their patients recovered their breath and were soon fighting off the restraint of their caring attendants.

For many years now, the St John's Ambulance Brigade has provided professional help for those hurt in battle. Serious injuries are less common than might be expected in such an unruly fracas. Hospital treatment is needed though for the occasional broken limb or collar bone or crushed ribs.

Eventually one side will gain the initiative. Once the scrum gets away from the brow of Hare Pie Bank, the progress for the more fortunate team is down hill. Their opponents then have the arduous task of fighting against the gradient and the weight of the pressing crowd as well as a re-invigorated opposition.

Mud and slush, dung and thorns add a certain character to this unusual game. A series of casualties, a few private fights and the settling of old scores are regarded as only minor distractions.

The famous Burrows family of Medbourne are seen in full action, 1964

A CONTINUING BRAWL

Sometimes after a breakaway there will be two separate scrums until one pile realises the bottle is elsewhere. Nothing daunted the struggle continues until a conclusive running break is made. If it is Medbourne's day, this is a long athletic sprint across low meadows, ahead of a few determined but failing opponents. If the bottle goes to Hallaton, the whole melee tumbles down the steep Tenters slope and into the brook. Last desperate attempts are made to rescue the situation, with Medbourne fighting gamely all the way through the stream. When the weather has been wet, the Tenters bank turns into one huge mud slide and the brook, swollen to bursting point, becomes a formidable obstacle. This makes for an even more impressive spectacle for those who brave the scene on a wet Easter Monday.

The scrum moves and bodies fall out. Limbo dancer to the right, Jillie Daisley to the left.

Once the first bottle has been won there is time for much needed refreshment. However the contest is approaching a critical point. The losers of the first bottle know they have to win now to stay in contention. Back up the hill to Hare Pie Bank come the contestants for the second bottle. The number of spectators has dwindled dramatically and many of the combatants may still be taking a break. There is no pageantry and little cheering or joviality this time. It is a serious fight. Pride is at stake, with the prospect of victory for one side and the dark spectre of defeat for the other.

"Bottle One, Bottle Two, Bottle Three". Three times into the air goes the bottle and immediately battle is resumed. Though with fewer players, the struggle is even more intense than before, with so much more at stake. The second bottle is the dummy. Being lighter, it is easier to carry on the run. Hence some "runners" may have been held back in reserve for the new assault.

THE CONTEST

Should the second bottle be won by the losers of the first bottle, a decider is required. The surviving battle-weary combatants drag themselves yet again, up the hill to Hare Pie Bank.

By now there are even fewer participants. They are supported by only a handful of spectators but this does nothing to detract from the intensity of the conflict. Limbs may ache, bruises may hurt, cuts may sting but passions run as high as ever. Up in the air three times goes the bottle and the final fight is under way. The players pile in, each striving for early possession to pass the bottle to waiting runners. With fewer bodies around movement is now less constrained. All the same plays are used as in the earlier battles but the third bottle tends to travel more speedily to the stream and to victory. As the contest ends, the gallant few remaining combatants, winners and losers alike, return as heroes.

L-R: David Benyon and Simon Bull emerge from Hallaton Brook , 1994

A Hallaton man named Tommy Tyler was a spectator down by the brook. Ascending the steep bank was too difficult for him as he had a wooden leg. Alas, he was caught up in the scrum and was tumbled into the brook, then in full spate. The buoyancy of his wooden leg and the strong current proved too much for him and he was carried off downstream and had to be rescued by others.

Tommy Tyler with his wooden leg sitting outside his house in Eastgate, C.1900

Everyone is hatted at this traditional victory celebration at the Buttercross, in front of the blacksmiths smithy and looking up High Street. The ladies superb Easter bonnets are a special feature on this cold early Easter Monday, 1901.

CELEBRATIONS

The battle has been fought, two bottles have been won and the contest is over. It may have taken as little time as two hours or as much as five hours to reach the conclusion. Whatever the result, the participants and supporters of both villages come back to Hallaton for the concluding ceremony. With cuts and bruises and aching limbs, the battle-weary combatants show all the signs of having engaged in a tough fight. The victors, now with renewed vigour, exchange exited tales of incidents and achievements. The losers sapped of all energy, come with good grace and a fierce determination to return for the battle next year and to win.

The victors and vanquished gather in good natured camaraderie around the Buttercross. The winning bottle is ceremonially uncorked. Now the man who won the first bottle is hoisted to the very top of the monument and sits astride the stone ball that forms the finial piece. His position is precarious but he can still manage to hold on to the bottle, now as a token of victory. Exultantly he raises the bottle high above his head, to the accompaniment of flashing cameras and a great cheer from the assembled crowd. To even more cheers he takes the bottle in both hands, holding it above his head he takes a substantial draught of the ale. The keg is thrown back down to his team members for them to drink to their success.

The battle churned ale is warm and unpalatable but after hours of fighting for it, the liquid is nectar to the victors. Players of both sides now join in the beer drinking as a reward for their efforts and three cheers are given for the losing side. The ceremonies over, the crowd disperses; some back to the pubs and on to an evening of revelries.

RECORDED HISTORY

England prospered during the Georgian period and the reigns of Queen Victoria and King Edward VII. It was a time of change for Hallaton and for its Easter Monday custom. Whilst many features of the traditions remained the same, others developed with the cultural, economic and social changes of the times.

EARLY PICTURES

Two early photographers have contributed greatly to our awareness of the history of the custom. Frederick Hawke was a remarkable man, whose inventiveness and entrepreneurial skills earned him a niche in Hallaton's history. Many of the pictures in this booklet are the result of his photography. These show the popularity of the event. Of particular note is the smartness of dress; the ladies' stunning Easter Bonnets, the men in tweeds and waistcoats. All wore hats. Clearly it was a time for dressing up; an occasion for Sunday best, a day of festivity.

Sir Benjamin Stone, the MP for East Birmingham, was a man of substance with a particular interest in local customs. A respected photographer, he travelled the world with his tripod and glass plate camera.

In 1905, Sir Benjamin visited Hallaton. He was immaculately dressed in frock coat, waistcoat, spats and a tall black silk top hat. All went well as he photographed the procession and the pageantry. When repeatedly he attempted to hold up the proceedings on Hare Pie Bank the crowd had had enough. One wag threw a missile at the elegant hat and knocked it off. Sir Benjamin was affronted and showed it, so prompting the jeering crowd to throw more missiles. Gathering his tripod and camera, he beat a hasty retreat in high dudgeon, never to return.

In the afternoon the principal officers collect the Hare Pie at the Rectory. L-R: Ted Wooley (railway worker), Edwin Ted Hawke (shoemaker), Omar Neal (carrier, grazier) custodian of the Bottles, Rev Canon Chetwynd Stapylton Rector of Hallaton, George Hill (blacksmith of Church Lane), Harry Neal (farm worker), 1905.

The surviving pictures from Sir Benjamin's visit show some interesting features. Most important is the evident prominence of the local Friendly Societies. Hallaton had two participating lodges of such bodies. The Friendlies were formed early in the nineteenth century. Their purpose was insurance. Each presented itself as a society, with much ceremony and status attached to it officers. The two lodges held their annual dinners at lunchtime on Easter Monday. The Hallaton Friendly met at The Old Royal Oak while the Oddfellows met at The Fox Inn. Their inclusion added much to the formality and the pageantry of the event.

HARE PIE, PENNY LOAVES AND ALE

The hare has been a symbol of Easter from pagan times. Its association with the custom at Hallaton is not surprising but has taken various forms.

The Hare Pie was recorded as part of the custom in the earliest reference but the hare has also played another significant role. In previous centuries a freshly killed hare was carried on a pole at the front of the procession. More appropriate to modern taste and attitudes, the real hare has been replaced by a beautiful bronze hare, finely sculptured by the celebrated Hallaton sculptor, Ken Ford.

The Hare Pie is substantial today but in the past it was huge. Indeed, records tell of two Hare Pies of great size and in some early documents they were said to contain forty pounds of English Beef. Other accounts give the fillings as veal and bacon but the earliest references mention only hare.

Vast crowds fill High Street before the Great War, 1913.

In many of the photographs the band can be seen as prominent in the procession. The band has long played an important rule on Easter Monday and it still does today. For many years, Hallaton boasted its own brass band. With gleaming brass and sporting smart uniforms the band was a fine spectacle and a reflection of village pride. The Bottle Kicking song "Old Easter Monday" was of course, an essential piece in their repertoire. As well as the Easter Monday duties, the band would have been called upon to play for fêtes and fairs, for special services and for public events.

The rector has always played an important role in the annual custom. It was his duty to take the service, give a relevant sermon and give his blessing to the event. Tradition also required the incumbent, with one of the richest livings in Leicestershire, to provide the Hare Pie, the Penny Loaves and the Ale. Not all rectors have been in favour: Long ago, one earned a place in village folklore.

Around 1789 the Revd. C. J. Bewicke, felt that the money that tradition required him to spend could be put to better use. He sought to put an end to the practice. This was seen as outrageous by the inhabitants who showed their resentment. Protests were made and a sinister message appeared on the rectory and church wall. Allegedly written in blood, it said: No Pie - No Parson!

Not surprisingly, the Rector, gave way and the Pies were duly provided.

The bung has been drawn from Omar Neal's bottle and the winner raises a glass of ale atop the Buttercross, C 1900.

Today we find that the provision of the Hare Pie, the Penny Loaves and the Ale is no longer assigned to the rector. Since 1962 it has become the responsibility of the organisers of the Bottle-Kicking.

The distribution of the Penny Loaves may have been necessary in earlier times but lapsed early in the 20th century. Some two hundred and fifty years ago a penny would have bought a substantial (1lb or 0.5 kg) loaf of bread. Indeed, in his History of Leicestershire, (1797) John Nichols gives an account of the Bottle Kicking and mentions that the penny loaves were cut into quarters. The tradition of the Penny Loaves was revived in the 1960's, restoring an important element of the Easter Monday custom

The Ale in the Bottles was welcome refreshment for the battle-weary participants but was hardly sufficient for every one involved. Hence the prize was probably shared between those who had co-operated in its winning. This surely would have added to the competitiveness and development of team spirit.

A celebratory drink of specially brewed Bottle Kicking Ale, after filling and sealing the bottles at the Bewicke Arms. L-R: Phil Allan, Neil Spiers (Landlord), David Wainwright, Simon Bull.

AN 18TH CENTURY ACCOUNT

Many articles refer to the Hallaton customs. Some are evidently plagiarised copies of descriptions by earlier writers. Others are original and worthy of examination. The most valuable description appears in The History of Leicestershire by John Nichols. In this we have an eye witness account of the event, written by a local yeoman farmer. It was John Tailby of Slawston, a man passionately interested in local history, who wrote to Nichols in 1796, the description that follows:

"An ancient annual Cuftom at Hallaton"

A piece of land was many years ago given, the rents and profits of which the rector for the time being was to receive for his own ufe, on condition of providing two Hare Pies, a quantity of Ale, and two dozen Penny Loaves, to be fcrambled for on Eafter Monday annually, after divine fervice and a fermon preached. The land, during the open field ftate, was called Hare Crop Leys, and when the inclofure took place on 1770, land was allotted to the rector in his allotment in lieu of the faid Hare Crop Leys.

The manner of fcrambling is thus: Two large Pies (which, inftead of Hares, are now made out of Veal and Bacon) arc made in raifed crufts at the rector's houfe; and, when baked, are cut into quarters or parts, and put into a fack: the Ale (now about two gallons) is put into wooden bottles, without handles or ftrings to hold them by, the corks well thruft in, and cut off clofe to the bottle mouths, and put into a fack alfo; the Penny Loaves are quartered and put in a bafket, which a man carries; as do two others the facks; when the proceffion begins, confifting of men, women, and children.

The fpot appropriated for the fcrambling for the Pies and Ale is about a quarter of a mile South of the town, a fmall oblong bank, 10 yards long and 6 wide; with a fmall old trench round it, and a

circular hole in the centre; and is called Hare-Pie Bank. After they have left the town, the man with the bread walks towards the Bank; and, as he proceeds, at times throws pieces of bread before him, which is eagerly caught by boys which furround him, the bread being all diftributed before they arrive at the fpot deftined for the fcrambling for the Pies and Ale.

As foon as the men with the facks arrive at the Bank, the Pies and Ale are tumbled promifcuoufly out of the facks into the hole in the centre, when a fcene of noife and confufion takes place, and bloody nofes and bruifed fingers are often the confequence: one will feize a piece of Pye, or a bottle of Ale; a fecond will trip up his heels, and fall upon him; and a third perhaps feize and

John Nichols the historian and proprietor of the Gentlemans Magazine.

keep possession of the prize, until a fourth ferves him with the fame; and fo on, until four or five fellows agree to form a party, and affift each other in bearing away the wifhed-for bottle to a convenient place, and there divide the fpoil. The afternoon is fpent in feftivity, ringing of bells, fighting of cocks, quoits and fuch like exercifes, by Hallaton and the neighbouring youth."

This excellent description is most helpful. In these and other writings many clues can be found to assist interpreting the past character of the custom.

AN EASTER REVELRY

By the end of the eighteenth century the event had developed into a well-defined holiday of fun and festivity. This was a feast day; a day of eating and drinking, a time for revelry and excitement. Clearly Easter Monday was also a day of jollification and games. In addition to the scrambling for Hare Pie and fighting for the Bottles of Ale there were many other activities, attractions and forms of entertainment. Undoubtedly the cock fighting mentioned by Tailby was a popular entertainment. No doubt it was but one of the opportunities for gambling. It seems that no chance was wasted to make the most of the celebrations that did not end with nightfall. The revels often continued into the night with drinking, music and dancing in the village pubs. Even longer lasting festivities have been reported. Around 1900, the Easter holiday extended into Tuesday, with organised races, prizes and entertainment arranged by village leaders.

Earlier accounts show that the scrambling for pie and ale was a free-for-all, with youths and men of Hallaton fighting each other. The individual combatant did not require a boundary but won his prize and took his winnings wherever he could. This may have been the pattern for centuries past. It was inevitable that in time, individualism would give way to co-operation. Players would learn to work in packs for greater effectiveness and a more certain share of the prize. Villagers would have collaborated in groups to better compete with other packs. Eventually the need for some kind of goal, end point or home would have been recognised, where the scrambling would end. The home stream at the bottom of the hill provided a natural and obvious boundary.

It is recorded that youths from neighbouring villages came to Hallaton to join the revelries; some from as far away as Desborough in Northamptonshire. The established packs from Hallaton surely would have regarded these strangers with hostility. Their presence would have served to unify as a village team, the hitherto separate gangs from Hallaton. Over a few years inter-village rivalry would have grown. Thus the basis for a Hallaton-Medbourne contest was laid.

Hallaton Band proudly pose outside the Fox Inn in 1864.

It is important to note that the records reveal no written mention of Medbourne in opposition to Hallaton until 1890. From those writings it is clear that Medbourne's involvement in the Bottle Kicking was already well established. What had been simply a Hallaton affair in the 1790's had developed as a Hallaton versus Medbourne contest by the 1850's. The event became a two-team battle, not by arrangement or decision but by the evolving behaviour and practice of the participants.

The lack of specific reference to Medbourne's role in earlier records does nothing to belittle or detract from the importance of the contribution of Medbourne to the event today and for its part over at least a century and a half.

EVOLVING PRACTICES

The Open Field system still existed in Hallaton until the end of the 18th century. So with few hedges to impede their progress, the combatants could exploit open country to get away with the bottle. Some of the rivals would pull in opposite directions, bringing a territorial element into the competition. The outsider opponents, perhaps mainly from Medbourne, needed a boundary at which they could claim a win. The Hallaton elders of the day may well have agreed to meet the need but must have selected the Medbourne stream as an equivalent boundary rather than as a fair one!

In the 1830's there were only two bottles. Imagine that Medbourne took one bottle over their stream while Hallaton won the other bottle. Honour would have been shared but there would have been no real winner. It is likely that the additional third bottle was introduced as a tie-breaker. The dummy bottle was porobably made in approximately 1830 by Jonathan Curtis, the Hallaton wheelwright. This economy version made of solid wood, does not need filling with ale. The rector who financed the event would surely have admired such thrift. The dummy soon became the second bottle of the contest, so keeping a bottle with undisturbed ale in reserve, to be used only if needed for a tie-break.

Towards the end of the 19th century the railways were being constructed. This involved large gangs of navigators, many of whom were Irish. Two distinct groups were working near Hallaton, one group building the tunnel and cuttings to the north and one group working on the embankments and tracks, mostly to the south. Away from home and with enforced holidays, the labourers eagerly joined in the Easter battle. As strangers with no roots in Hallaton, some supported Hallaton and some played for Medbourne. The increase of manpower must have added to the excitement and no doubt, to the contention.

The building of roads and railways had a profound effect on the villages and on attendance at the Bottle Kicking. Travel was

The Warrener, John Morison at the Buttercross displaying the fine bronze hare springing from a sheaf of wheat ears, symbolising fertility and replacing the old custom of tying a real hare to the top of the pole. The hare was created by Ken Ford, the Hallaton sculptor in 1994.

no longer a privilege of the wealthy but available to all. By the beginning of the 20th century there were rail and charabanc excursions to Hallaton from all directions. With these developments, it was inevitable that the recognition of the event would increase. From being a quaint local custom, the Hare Pie Scrambling & Bottle Kicking evolved into an event of county wide and national interest.

The custom underwent substantial development in the nineteenth century. What had been an annual tussle between Hallaton lads, had become a popular spectacle with an organised contest between the two villages. The Hare Pie was a common feature throughout. The association of the hare with Easter seems to have been the earliest and most enduring feature of this ancient custom of Hare Pie Scrambling and Bottle Kicking.

ORIGINS OF HALLATON'S STRANGE CUSTOM

MYTHS AND EVIDENCE

The earliest written references to Hare Pie Scrambling & Bottle Kicking yet discovered are dated 1698. Other papers of the 18th century refer to the "ancient custom" at Hallaton, thus confirming that the event had a much earlier origin. To delve further back is difficult without specific records. However, progress can be made by testing the legends and traditions against the evidence of other historical records. Something of the distant past of the custom and how it subsequently developed can be inferred.

ENCLOSURES

The year 1771 was a turning point in Hallaton's history. The feudal manorial system was undergoing rapid change. A new style of agriculture was being established. Most dramatic was the complete change of the very landscape. By the Enclosure Award, almost the whole of Hallaton's three thousand acres was subjected to a redesign.

New roads were cut, paths were set out and land was re-allocated. The dozens of fields seen today were created by the sub-division of the three huge open fields of medieval Hallaton. The objective of enclosures was to improve the efficiency of farming by changing from arable to livestock farming with cattle and sheep. For farmers this meant higher profits and for the government it increased food production to feed the growing urban population.

This monumental upheaval had a profound effect on the whole community and not least on the Hare Pie Scrambling & Bottle Kicking. The most obvious and welcome change was that the land to be fought over was no longer ploughed land. As grassland for grazing there was no longer the risk of crop damage by the bottle-kickers. The second change was the introduction of many new hedges where none had existed. Where earlier combatants had enjoyed clear and open country over which to run with

Glebe Terrier of south Rectory taken in 1698 showi[ng] land held at Hare Croft Furlong, St Morrell's Wel[l,] Tenters Furlong, Chapel Way and Hare Pie Bank.

THE LEGEND OF THE HARE

There is a much-quoted legend that every small child of Hallaton learns and passes on to the next generation. Quoted by journalists and historians, past and present, by locals and outsiders each telling contains the same essentials. The story goes:

Long, long ago, two ladies were crossing a field when alas, they were chased by a bull. The women were doomed as the bull rapidly closed on them. At the very last moment however, a hare started in their path, distracting the bull and so deflecting its charge. Thanks to the hare, the ladies escaped from what would surely have been a severe goring and likely death.

The legend continues:

The ladies were so relieved at their miraculous delivery that, as well as giving thanks to God in prayer, they made a tangible thanksgiving. They donated, to the rector of the parish, the rents of the furlong known as Hare Crop Leys. They made it a condition that the rector should provide annually two hare pies, two dozen penny loaves and a quantity of ale. He was required also, on each Easter Monday, to offer a service and preach a sermon.

Such stories are subject to embellishments in successive tellings. Distinguishing fact from fiction is difficult but some incident must have given rise to the persistent legend. Despite a lack of hard proof there is good corroborative evidence noted below, that strongly supports the legend.

Until 1962, the hare pies, loaves and ale were provided by the rector. It is unlikely that any rector would have contributed unless there had been a sound basis to the requirement.

References to Hare Crop Leys and to Hare Pie Bank appeared in 1797, in the History & Antiquities of Leicestershire, by John Nichols.

In the Enclosure Award of 1771, the Hallaton rector was given Parson's Leys, land in lieu of Hare Crop Leys.

Early ecclesiastical records indicate the receipt of a bequest of land at Hare Crop Leys.

Map by William Kip showing the importance of Hallaton in Elizabethan times, from an original survey by Christopher Saxton in 1576.

their kegs of ale, they now had quickthorn hedges to impair progress. With sheep and cattle now grazing in the fields, provision had to be made for immediate repair of broken hedges and fences. That need continues.

Prior to enclosure Hallaton had the traditional three-field system with huge fields, each of about 850 acres. The vast fields were cultivated in recognised patches, rather like a block of allotments. Each cultivated block, known as a furlong, was given a name and sub-divided into separately owned strips but all cultivated with the same crop. It was the persistent pattern of ploughing of these strips that gave rise to the ridges and furrows still visible today. The names of ancient furlongs still used today include Hare Pie Bank, The Tenters, St Morrell's Well, Stowe Close and Bean Hill. These names give us clues to the early existence of Hare Pie Scrambling & Bottle Kicking and pointers to the origins of the custom.

A comprehensive survey of manorial lands was made by John Wing in 1707. The survey contains references to Hare Pie Bank. The naming of the land must have followed the practice of Hare Pie Scrambling.

Evidence also comes from earlier records of land sales and leases. The attached "field terriers", show the names and locations of the furlongs and even the ownership of the individual strips of land. Glebe terriers, for the Hallaton rectory land, date back to 1606.

The land allocated to provide for the Hare Pie, Bread and Ale was called Hare Crop Leys. The word Leys shows that this furlong of flat, low-lying land was reserved for grazing. A plan only recently discovered has identified the precise location of Hare Crop Leys. It lies to the Southwest of Love Lane, the fieldroad to Slawston. It was perhaps here that the legendary ladies were walking when the grazing Village Bull broke its tether. The rest of the story has become the very stuff of legend.

Whatever existed before the 17th century, the custom would have received a substantial boost with the bequest of Hare Crop Leys to provide hare pies, bread and ale. The evidence fits well with the old tale of the two ladies and their miraculous escape from the bull.

WHY HARE PIE BANK?

The antiquity of Hallaton, or Halloughton as it was also known, is not in doubt. It has been occupied by the Romans, the Vikings, the Anglo-Saxons. The stunning mound of Castle Hill and the arches of the church are lasting evidence of the Norman presence in Hallaton. Along the south bank of the stream undeveloped ground rises steeply to the prominent hilltop known as Hare Pie Bank. Only a quarter of a mile from the village, Hare Pie Bank was an obvious location for gatherings, for games and rituals. It is easy to imagine young farm workers on a religious holiday, in boisterous high spirits, larking about on the hilltop, and eventually tumbling an old wheel hub back to the village.

There are two routes up this hill. A medieval pathway known as Tenters runs from the village green up the hill, and the thousand year old road of Bride Hill leading from the church.

Deeds and terriers expose more about the land around these two routes. Between the steep slopes of Tenters and Bride Hill is a piece of land recorded in the 17th and 18th centuries as Stowe Close. In a charter deed of 1318, it was known as Stowe Well. According to experts in place-names, the name Stowe derives from Stoe, which in

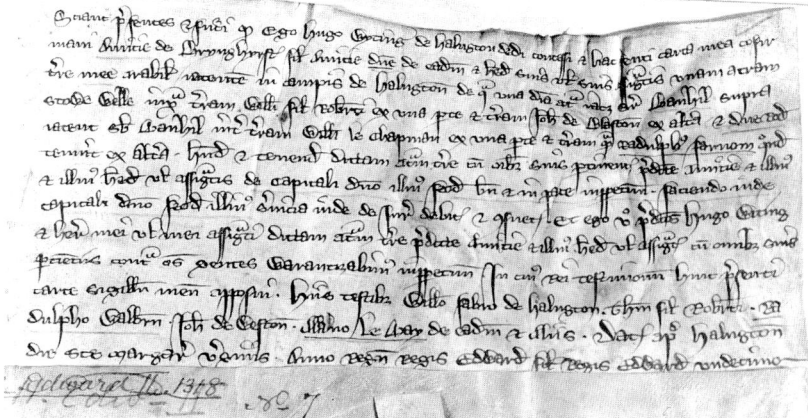

Charter Deed dated 13th July 1318 confirms both the existence and position of Stowe Well.

Old English means a meeting place, particularly one having religious and festive connections. Here then is evidence that the field on the hill above the village was being used for festive and religious gatherings in the 14th century, just as it is today on each Easter Monday! The field is still known as Stowe Close.

There is recent support for these interpretations. Dr Graham Jones of Leicester University announced in 1998 the discovery of the existence at Hallaton of a shrine to St Morrell. Though a little known saint in England today, this saint was the focus of a cult that built up in France in the 11th and 12th centuries. In his will dated 1532, Rev. Sir Francis Butler the rector of Hallaton, left money for his curate to go on a pilgrimage. The stations of the pilgrimage included Our Lady of Walsingham and the Shrine of St Morrell at Hallaton. Adding to this is the evidence of a furlong named St Morrell and a holy well known as St Morrell's Well. Research confirms that St Morrell's furlong adjoins or is indeed part of Stowe Close. The names St Morrell's Well and Stowe Well refer to the same well, which in reporting, may have acquired its two different names, one from its location and another name from its dedication. A key piece of evidence comes from a document from around 1600, from the Lincoln Diocesan archives, confirming that the Chapel to St Morrell stood on what we now know as Hare Pie Bank.

The story of St Morrell (St Maurille in French) 363-453AD is interesting and colourful. He was a monk ordained by St Martin who ultimately became the Bishop of Angers in the Loire. Over the centuries, many churches and chapels in France were dedicated in his name. It is quite likely that a Norman family settling here would have wished to respect their own Saint in their new surroundings. Of those closely associated with Hallaton Robert Crevequer or Ralph Martival are the two most likely to have established the chapel to St Morrell in Hallaton, 1150-1250AD

A 14thCentury mural in Angers Cathedral depicts Bishop Morrell declining to baptise the baby Renatus, later the subject of his most famous miracle.

Thus we have evidence at Hare Pie Bank, of a nearby Holy Well and Stowe Close, St Morrell's furlong and the associated shrine and chapel to St Morrell. All this confirms that Hare Pie Bank and the adjoining land was the site of religious and festive gatherings for at least 800 years.

BACK THROUGH TIME

Hare Pie Bank was once a place of religious significance. How much association there is between the spiritual rites of the 1st millennium and the Hare Pie and Bottle Kicking Scrambling of the 2nd millennium is a matter of speculation but there is evidence of strong links.

The footpath from Hallaton via Tenters to Hare Pie Bank was once known as Chapel Way. The word "chapel" appears also in deeds for adjacent pieces of land. The raised earthworks at the top of Hare Pie Bank exhibit a rectangle, the size and proportions for the footings of a small building. With its proximity to St Morrell's Well, this is further convincing evidence that St Morrell's Chapel, referred to in the Lincoln Diocesan documents, was on the top of Hare Pie Bank where the annual scrambling begins. The ritual use of the religious site could have continued and eventually become the Easter custom as it is now known.

The religious associations of the site may well have preceded the building of the Chapel. An extension of the evidence suggests that the origin of Hare Pie Scrambling was pagan. The Hare itself, a prominent part of the Hallaton custom, was always regarded as a special creature. Ancient man would have wondered at the curious behaviour of hares in the Spring and attached to them a great significance. It was held that : -

To catch a hare on Easter Monday is to be blessed with good fertility in the forthcoming year.

No doubt this related to animal and crop abundance as well as to human fecundity. The parading of the hare, its sacrifice and inclusion in the Hare Pie are indications of early beliefs that may well pre-date Christianity. Even the Easter Bunny of the 20th century may be a sanitised version of the ancient sacrifice of the hare.

The Hallaton custom takes place on Easter Monday. Easter of course, is the most

L-R: The Revd John Adams and the venerable Michael Edson the Archdeacon of Leicester share a joke and a pint at the Fox Inn, on Easter Monday, 1994.

holy religious festival in the Christian calendar: It is also the beginning of Spring. This time of new life and growth was celebrated long before England was converted to Christianity. The term Easter derives from Eastre, (Eostre, Oestre or Ester), the name of the pagan goddess of fertility.

Long before Christianity came to Hallaton it is likely that the hare was sacrificed as a fertility rite, to the goddess Eastre. It is conceivable that early pagan sacrificial ceremonies took place on Hare Pie Bank for many centuries. The hill acquired the name "Stoe" signifying a place of religious gatherings. Then came the conversion to Christianity. The Christian church has often incorporated pagan customs into its own ceremonies, not opposing what exists but adapting and effectively Christianising practices it could not condone.

The religious context faded, the killings were abandoned but the customs continued. The Church blessed rather than berated the seemingly unChristianlike behaviour, that is a form of sacrifice still practised in the 21st century as Hare Pie Scrambling.

CONCLUSIONS
EVIDENCE BASED INFERENCES

A respected and knowledgeable descendant of an ancient Hallaton family, farmer John Eaton said "No one knows and nobody will ever know". This was the response in the 1990s to a TV interviewer who asked "How did the Bottle Kicking start?" John Eaton may have been right in the sense that there was no point in time when it all started. What is now understood as the result of the Morison research, is that the custom developed as the progressive combination of several elements. Each element has its own history and leaves some scattered particles of related evidence from which inferences can be drawn.

The pagan fertility rites with the hare may have been practised for many centuries before Hallaton's history was ever recorded. Originally, those rites would have been in secret as a sacrificial ceremony for the religious hierarchy, meeting at the revered meeting place at the top of the hill. Gradually the ceremony evolved as a public celebration of the coming of Spring, with a

The massed crowds surge past the church on their way to Hare Pie Bank, 1898.

parade to the special site, the place of the sacrifice. The parade of the Hare on a Pole and the sharing of Hare Pie are surely the civilised successors of darker practices.

St Morrell, a revered saint in France, was honoured in Norman England. His shrine at Hallaton was a place of pilgrimage. An established religious site on the top of a hill, near to St Morrell's Well, was an appropriate place to erect St Morrell's chapel. It did not survive and may have been destroyed in the

The Rev Thomas Preece cuts the Hare Pie outside the Rectory front door, with a very smartly dressed audience, 1910.

29

reformation. The earthwork is tangible evidence that aligns with the recently discovered evidence of the association of Hallaton with the 4th century St. Morrell.

The distribution of bread and ale was almost certainly an extension of an established Easter Monday ceremony. Such charitable gifts to the poor have abounded over the ages. The bequest by the two ladies of legend fits easily into the theory of a gradually developing custom. The records in deeds and land terriers support the story of the ladies, the bull and the hare and infer that the incident occurred before 1600.

Jostling for pieces of pie or bread was inevitable. A brawl would be certain to ensue as the young men tried to grasp the kegs of ale. Thus the intended sharing of the ale had in time become a battle between competing youths of the village. The event took on much of the character of present-day Bottle Kicking much later, as the men from Medbourne joined the fray. The contest became a fight, not amongst Hallaton men but between the villagers of Hallaton and Medbourne.

From its beginnings in unrecorded history, the Easter Monday custom has evolved and adapted. For many centuries the Hare Pie Scrambling and Bottle Kicking has continued, substantially in the form in which the strange custom is conducted into the 21st century.

Long may the history and the tradition continue.

POSTSCRIPT

Inevitably in a reconstruction spanning hundreds of years there are bound to be areas of uncertainty. With many legends, plenty of theories and a dearth of real knowledge we have had to make assumptions. We draw conclusions on the basis of the limited evidence available to us today. The authors are conscious that several of the aspects raised warrant more research. As time passes, we hope that more information will come to light so that we or those who follow, will be able to fill in more pieces of this intriguing jigsaw puzzle.

JVM, PAD

The winning Hallaton team pose on the banks of Hallaton brook at Sandybrook. The water pumping system shed can be seen in the background.

PRINCIPAL PARTICIPANTS IN 1999

Master of the Stowe	Phil (Pinny) Allan
Custodian of the Bottles	David (Wacka) Wainwright
Bottle Carriers	Michael Hunt
	Simon Bull
Warrener with Hare	John Morison
Hare Pie Carriers	Julie Allan
	Liz Hines
Penny Loaves Carrier	Gill Clayton
Rector of Hallaton	Rev John Richardson
Medbourne representative	John Burrows
Hare Pie cooked by	Julie Allan
Penny Loaves baked by	Cathy Morison
The Fox Inn Landlord	Ricki Varela
The Bewicke Arms Landlord	Neil Spiers

FURTHER READING

Billson C J	County Folklore 1895
Brand J	Observations on Popular Antiquities 1795 & 1841
Drake-Carnell FJ	Old English Customs & Ceremonies 1938
Dyer T F T	British Popular Customs 1911
Lones T E	British Calendar Customs 1936
Morison & Daisley	Hallaton, Hare Pie Scrambling & Bottle Kicking 2000
Nichols J	Nichols History of Leicestershire 1797

All rights reserved. No part of this publication may be reproduced, stored in a retrieval system, or transmitted in any form or by any means, electronic, mechanical, photocopying, recording or otherwise, or lent, resold, hired out or circulated, without prior permission of the copyright owner. The moral rights of the authors have been asserted.

Design by Ivan Morison, D & D Ltd, Birmingham, UK.
Printed by R & G Designs Ltd, Leicester, UK.
Published by Hallaton Museum Press, 8 Churchgate, Hallaton, Leicestershire LE16 8TY, UK.
Copyright John Morison 2000
ISBN 0-9538393-0-3
Produced with financial assistance from Awards For All Lottery Grants for Local Groups.

The publisher makes no representation, express or implied, with regard to the accuracy of the information contained in this book and cannot accept any legal responsibility or liability for any errors or omissions that may be made. Every effort has been made to trace the holders of copyright materials used in this publication. Should any omissions become apparent, the publishers will make the necessary arrangements at the first opportunity.

Many photographs in this book have been loaned by local residents, both past and present, for publication, and we are indebted to them for allowing their publication. We should also like to extend our thanks to the various organisations that have granted permission to reproduce other copyright materials.
Photographic credits: Frederick Hawke: Cover, page 5, 6B, 9B, 11, 12, 16B, 17, 19, 20A, 29A, 29B, 30. Sir Benjamin Stone: page 4, 18. Paul Ferraby: page 1. John Morison: page 3, 7B, 13B, 16A, 20B, 25, 26, 27, 28, 31. Peter Suffolk: page 6A, 15. Unknown: Page 21, 22. Market Harborough Museum: Page 8, 9A, 10 13A. The Brewers Society: page 7A, 14. Ansel Dunham: Page 23. Leicestershire Record Office: page 24,26. Service Régional de l'Inventaire Général: page 27.

ALSO AVAILABLE FROM HALLATON MUSEUM PRESS

HALLATON, HARE PIE SCRAMBLING & BOTTLE KICKING

NEW RELEAS

- First Edition Hardback Over 150 Pages
- The only book on Hallaton's strange and ancient custom
- What really happened on Hare Pie Bank?
- How exactly did Hare Pie Scrambling and Bottle Kicking evolve?
- Is the legend of the two ladies and the bull true?
- The stories behind the myth and the legend
- Who was Hallaton's St Morrell?
- Why did Alice Neville give King John 200 hens that she might lie one night with her husband?
- Why was Lord Bardolf hung, drawn and quartered, with his head set on a spike on the gates of Lincoln?
- A fascinating insight into Hallaton's dark history
- What do a terrier, a hawk, a stone and a hunting vicar all have in common?
- What or who was the Leaden Lover?
- Which existing Hallaton families are mentioned in the Domesday Book of 1086?

The answers to these and many other questions are all to be found in this cornucopia of a book, covering Hallaton's strange and ancient custom on Easter Monday and tales from the lives of its inhabitants.

By John Morison and Peter Daisley
Published by Hallaton Museum Press
ISBN 0-9538393-1-1